Suzy Zeus
Gets
Organized

SUZY ZEUS GETS ORGANIZED

MAGGIE ROBBINS

A

TIN HOUSE

BLOOMSBURY

BOOK

Judy—
You got me involved in my
first committee at St Lukes / St.
Jude's— which is pretty
much what kept me here
and led to...
all this.
With my
thanks +
LOVE,
Maggie

A Tin House/Bloomsbury Book

Published by Bloomsbury Publishing, New York and London
Distributed to the trade by Holtzbrinck Publishers

All papers used by Bloomsbury Publihsing are natural, recyclable products made from wood grown in well-managed forests. The manufacturing processes conform to the environmental regulations of the country of origin.

Library of Congress Cataloging-in-Publication Data has been applied for.

ISBN 1-58234-535-X
ISBN-13 9781582345352

First U.S. Edition 2005

10 9 8 7 6 5 4 3 2 1

Printed in the United States of America
by Quebecor World Fairfield

For Andrew

CONTENTS

We live for those who love us ...

—from a verse carved on the bells of
the Shrine Church of Our Lady of Solace,
Coney Island

CHAPTER 1
Suzy in Queens

SUZY ZEUS SETS SOME LIMITS

Suzy Zeus likes guys with handguns.
Suzy Zeus likes beer in kegs.
Suzy Zeus likes breaking windows.
Suzy Zeus likes breaking eggs.
Suzy's got a boyfriend, Harry.
Touch him and she'll break your legs.

Suzy likes her sister's undies.
Suzy likes her brother Keith.
Suzy likes her father's buck knife.
Suzy likes its leather sheath.
Suzy likes her boyfriend Harry.
Touch him and she'll break your teeth.

Suzy hails from Indiana,
land of crops, of Fords and farms.
Suzy lives in New York City,
land of cops and car alarms.
Suzy lives six blocks from Harry.
Touch him and she'll break your arms.

Suzy's got a kick-ass system.

Suzy is what Suzy owns.

Elton John and Cyndi Lauper,

Fleetwood Mac, the Rolling Stones

(Harry grooves to Waylon Jennings—

touch him and she'll break your bones),

Carly Simon, Sheena Easton,

Wham!, the Roches, Yes, *The Rose*,

Billy Joel, Duran Duran, and

Handel oratorios.

Harry's humming "My Sharona."

Touch him and she'll break your nose.

Suzy's got a bag of bridge mix.

Suzy's got some frozen peas.

Suzy's got a front-door dead bolt.

Harry's got a set of keys.

Harry's got a way with women.

Touch him and she'll break your knees.

Suzy stands before the mirror:

sultry, soulful, calm, complete.

Suzy loves her shapely shoulders,

likes her nose, adores her feet.
Wants a pair of mules in puce, a
pair of pumps in parakeet.

Harry asks her what she's up to.
Asks her almost every night.
Harry likes to see her naked,
see her naked in the light.
Harry never takes her dancing.
Harry says her hair's a fright.

Suzy Zeus is drinking whiskey.
Suzy Zeus is making eyes.
Suzy Zeus is making trouble
at the bar, with other guys.
Harry finds her, rips her dress off,
leaves it bunched around her thighs.

Suzy's got a can of bean dip.
Suzy's got a can of mace.
Suzy's got a Good News Bible.
Suzy's got a real nice place.
Harry's pissing out the window.
Touch him and she'll break your face.

SUZY CLEANS UP

Suzy tried to fix her vacuum,
found a bag for empty cans,
drained the sink and rinsed the dishes,
wiped the pot and both the pans.
That was it for pressing details.
That was it for weekend plans.

Suzy rented *Reefer Madness*,
thinking it was Jacques Cousteau.
Now she's lying on the sofa
—feeling quite adagio—
flipping through a *Car & Driver*,
slurping down a sloppy joe.

Louie's Lonesome Diner beckons—
Suzy's taking Lisa's shift.
Lisa's getting married Sunday.
Suzy needs a card and gift.
Yeah, the mini—Suzy's getting
off at two, she'll want a lift.

Harry's nuts for almond cookies.
Suzy buys him chocolate chip.
Harry has to work on weekends.
Suzy phones the dealership.
Harry's always with a client.
Harry says they'll take a trip.

Suzy wants her own small business.
Suzy wants her own backyard.
Suzy wants her own Jacuzzi.
Suzy needs a gift and card.
She'll become the Lonesome's owner,
queen of Northern Boulevard.

Lisa's theme is Hearts and Cupid.
Lisa's dress is long and nice.
Suzy thinks the whole thing's stupid.
Suzy said she'd bring the rice.
Suzy wouldn't marry Harry.
Maybe if he asked her twice.

SUZY TAKES THE WHEEL

Suzy loves her manly boyfriend,
loves him in the here and now.
Suzy loves his manly features.
Suzy loves his manly brow.
Suzy wants to love forever.
Touch her, tease her, tell her how.

Suzy wants to oil her body,
loose her hair and lose her head.
Harry hasn't phoned since Tuesday.
Could be missing, could be dead.
Suzy wants to love forever.
Touch her, tie her to the bed.

Suzy's going to have it easy.
Suzy's going to have it all.
Suzy's feeling bold and breezy.
Suzy isn't going to call.
Suzy wants to love forever.
Touch her, take her down the hall.

Suzy's in her favorite sweater.
Suzy's in her favorite dive.
Men keep buying Suzy bourbon.
Men keep Suzy Zeus alive.
Suzy wants to live forever.
Touch her, try her, let her drive.

SUZY TAKES A TRIP

Suzy Zeus went home for Christmas.
Suzy took a Trailways bus.
Locked herself inside the toilet.
Thought about her brother Gus.
Suzy sat there half an hour.
Driver didn't make a fuss.

Suzy's mom strung up the lightbulbs.
Suzy's mom put out the crèche.
Keith put Joseph humping Mary.
Suzy's mom said Keith was fresh.
Suzy's mom wants Christmas spirit.
Suzy's dad just wants some flesh.

Suzy's mom is always humming.
Suzy's dad is always right.
Suzy's mom is hard of hearing.
Suzy's dad stayed out all night.
Suzy's mom said not to worry.
Suzy's mom said not to fight.

Suzy Zeus threw up all morning,
lay in bed with Ed, the dog,
flipping through the late-November
Neiman Marcus catalog.
Liked the mango pedal pushers.
Liked the big ceramic frog.

Sally loves the sing-along they
have at church on Christmas Eve.
Suzy sat with Keith beside her,
Sally with her husband, Steve.
Gus will sit where Gus is put—just
get him when it's time to leave.

Suzy brought her mom a hot pad.
Suzy bought her dad some booze.
Gave her sister body lotion.
Keith she gave a rack of cues.
Keith gave her an ankle bracelet.
Suzy didn't ask him whose.

SUZY TAKES HER TIME

Suzy lost her plastic change purse.
Suzy lost at Truth or Dare.
Suzy lost her job at Louie's.
Suzy doesn't really care.
Suzy wants to buy an ear cuff.
Suzy wants to bleach her hair.

Louie's Lone was not a picnic.
Louie's laugh was very crude.
Suzy never liked the people.
Suzy never liked the food.
Suzy wants to waitress mornings.
Suzy wants to get tattooed.

Louie never fixed the heating.
Suzy never liked the cook.
Never liked the vinyl seating,
never liked the Wild West look.
Had to watch policemen eating.
Had no time to read a book.

Harry says she needs the money.

Harry—he can go to hell.

Suzy tells him she can dig up

rings and things that she can sell.

Suzy's doing what she wants to.

Doing nicely! Doing well.

Harry's making vodka Jell-O.

Suzy's got a jug of wine.

Harry says she'll need the money.

Harry wants to 69.

Suzy'd rather rent a thriller.

Suzy Zeus is doing fine.

SUZY REFUSES

Suzy's breath is deep and hot. Her
eyes are slits, her pupils specks.
Suzy's shredding all his tapes, his
shirts, the sheets where they had sex.
Harry, "just to save some cash," is
"crashing" with his high school ex.

Suzy Zeus told Harry never.
Suzy Zeus told Harry no.
Watched him phone to book a Honda,
watched him pack, and watched him go.
Suzy's full of ways she can sur-
prise this highway Romeo.

Harry said, a place to sleep in,
Harry said, to break the trip.
Harry said to stop her griping.
Harry said to get a grip.
Suzy makes it very messy
when her boyfriends double dip.

SUZY MOVES ON

Suzy Zeus is catching fire.
Suzy Zeus is catching rays.
Suzy Nairs her legs and armpits.
Suzy fasts and Suzy prays.
Suzy wants a better boyfriend—
one who's smarter, one who stays.

One who listens, one who loves her,
one who needs her, one who knocks.
Not like Harry, banging in and
tripping on his dirty socks.
By the time he says he's sorry,
Suzy will have changed the locks.

Suzy's taking off her panties.
Suzy's taking off some weight.
Suzy's putting on mascara.
Suzy's going on a date.
Suzy knows the girl for Harry
is a girl he can inflate.

SUZY MOURNS

Suzy's happy! Suzy's swell! She's
wise and pretty! Strong and free!
Ready for the taste and smell of
skin that sings and hands that see.
Suzy wakes at five. Or four. It
gives her extra energy.

Harry wasn't much to lose—a
skunk, a drunk, a blank, a bore.
Suzy Zeus has gotten over
tons of guys like him before!
Suzy shows them what she's made of.
Suzy shows them all the door.

Suzy's been with lots of people.
Suzy's had a lot of flings.
Only Harry called her "girlfriend,"
cared enough to clip her wings.
Suzy doesn't think about it.
When she does, it kind of stings.

Suzy thinks of Bobby, Brandon,
Chuckie, Stuckey, Burns, and Brad.
Purlis, Joey, Jetson, Killer,
Craig and Sil—Sudan and Chad.
Harry's free to play the field, girls.
Touch him. It's the latest fad.

CHAPTER 2
Suzy in Between

SUZY SETTLES IT

Suzy's station goes to static
as they play her favorite song.
Suzy's never had it easy—
now she's queasy all day long.
Six A.M.—she feels like she's been
eating something very wrong.

Longer grow the winter daytimes.
Shorter grow the winter nights.
No more bets on three-card Harry.
No more fibbing, no more fights.
Suzy prices string bikinis.
Suzy shoplifts fishnet tights.

Suzy severs yes from maybe,
will from could, and gets a beer.
No one wants an ugly baby.
No one wants a baby here.
Suzy walks along the river,
listens to a still, small cheer.

one, two, four, eight
who you are is who you date

two, four, eight, sixteen
who you are is what you've seen

eight, sixteen, thirty-two
who you are is what you do

thirty-two, sixty-four
spill you spill you on the floor

one hundred twenty-eight
who you are is what you hate

two hundred fifty-six
who you are is what you fix

SUZY RELATES

Someone set off bottle rockets
in the hallway as a joke.
Suzy saw her upstairs neighbor's
purple lipstick through the smoke.
Black-haired bony Bitterino
asked her in. They had a Coke.

Bitterino does some acting,
weekends with a downtown group.
Keeps a hatchet in her bedroom,
keeps her hair slicked back with goop.
Bitterino has a bedtime,
and a thing for Betty Boop.

Bitterino talks in riddles.
Bitterino talks in code.
Suzy's deep-dish apple pie, but
Bitterino's à la mode.
Bitterino has a club act.
Plans to take it on the road.

Bitterino's boots unbuckle.
Bitterino loves to bake.
Both her sheets are pure Egyptian,
like the pharoahs'—nothing fake.
Two alarm clocks: one is news, the
other rock. She's so awake.

Bitterino doesn't worry.
Bitterino doesn't yawn.
Bitterino asked her how her
nights were now, with Harry gone.
Suzy used up all the Kleenex.
Suzy talked till after dawn.

Bitterino filled their teacups.
Gave her bags of tea to keep.
Bitterino asked if there was
something hurting way down deep.
Suzy reached for Bitterino.
Bitterino said to sleep.

SUZY RELEASES

Suzy's going to walk on water.
Suzy's going to harrow hell.
Suzy's going to write a screenplay.
Suzy's going to learn to spell.
Suzy has forgotten him! The
best revenge is living well.

Suzy, now a strobe light, with her
every second passing strange,
jogs for seven hours straight, a-
round a late-night driving range.
Watching golf balls arc in darkness,
paths blown wild by winds of change.

Suzy wants to make it formal:
Harry's Most Disgusting Trait.
Makes a total list to choose from—
eighty-six? No, eighty-eight.
Bitterino serves her brunch. Ar-
ranges parsley on the plate.

SUZY BONDS

Bitterino does graffiti—
Bitterino bungee jumps.
Suzy can't get oatmeal smooth, but
Bitterino likes the lumps.
Bitterino's had the measles.
Suzy's only had the mumps.

Bitterino loves the ferry.
Bitterino loves the spray.
Bitterino stands in front and,
as they start, yells "Fuckin' A!"
When they sailed to Staten Island,
Bitterino said she'd pay.

SUZY BOLTS

Suzy Zeus is tense as stemware,
not explosive, just on edge—
needs a ten-foot wall around her,
or at least a ten-foot hedge.
Suzy's straining, teeth to toenails,
easing backward on the ledge.

Suzy wants a Chevy Nova.
Suzy wants an indoor pool.
Wants a town house just like Barbie's.
Suzy Zeus is no one's fool.
Suzy Zeus is no one's plaything,
no one's chattel, no one's tool.

Suzy's going to hit the highway,
find a lake or mountain glen.
Suzy thinks, Who needs a guidebook?
Doesn't every state have men?
She can buy a car on credit.
She can go beyond her Ken.

Suzy needs a long vacation.

Suzy needs to get away.

Suzy isn't liking liking.

Finding there's so much to say.

Suzy finds the difference striking.

Suzy finds it not okay.

CHAPTER 3
Suzy at Large

Donnez-moi your telephone number
Donnez-moi your Sunday afternoons
Donnez-moi a new way of wishing
and a coupon for stainless steel spoons

Donnez-moi a reason to visit
Donnez-moi a reason to stay
Donnez-moi a new way of wishing
and I'll donnez-vous a place in my day

There's a wink in your skin
and the places you go
There's a wild to your neck
I'd like to know— know— know—

Donnez-moi your heaviest sweater
Donnez-moi your highest shelf
Donnez-moi a new way of wishing
And I'll donnez-vous a place in myself

There's a spell in your voice
and a slow in your hair
There's a stretch of your neck
I'd like to wear— wear— wear—

SUZY TRIES THE OPEN ROAD

Suzy is avoiding radar,
breaking limits, passing wrecks.
Suzy Zeus's passing fancy
is to meet a guy named Tex,
drive like hell on long straight highways,
stop five times a day for sex.

Suzy stretches, rolls her shoulders—
breathing deep, surveys the scene.
Suzy eats a biscuit breakfast
at a place called Brendalene.
Suzy loves amazing Graceland.
Suzy thinks the King is keen.

Deep in Memphis Suzy meets an
actor with a little pot.
Suzy's missed his Elvis, but he
tells her that "upstairs they got
fifteen minutes of vibrations—
just two quarters in the slot."

Suzy strolls through old New Orleans—
breezy jazz and moonlit views.
Someone says he'll show her heaven.
What on earth's she got to lose?
Every block a new adventure.
Every street another muse.

At a truck stop several drivers
let her know she drives real well.
"Want to park an eighteen-wheeler?"
asks a cute one. What the hell?
Lets the guy explore her caverns.
Lets him ring her Taco Bell.

SUZY LIKES THE OPEN ROAD

Suzy's passing through where Papa
lived when he was just a pup.
Stops for pie, and maybe coffee—
sure, she'll have another cup.
Suzy's speeding where the roadkill
comes with armor and rolls up.

Suzy traps a small familiar.
Maybe it's a great horned toad.
Chants through Kokonino County,
beds where once a river flowed.
Suzy, sacred, watches out for
miracles along the road.

At Four Corners, can she do it?
What she's always yearned to do?
All four limbs in different states? She
asks the forest ranger, Lou.
When they're done, she needs a shower.
Needs another T-shirt, too.

Suzy made a mad hegira,
took a chance, indulged a whim,
slept in Truth or Consequences,
shouted from the canyon's rim.
Harry said he'd show her Vegas.
It's still Vegas—who needs him?

SUZY EXPERIMENTS

Suzy wants a real explosion—
hears L.A. is into size.
Comes across an ad signed "Matthew."
Cannot know unless she tries.
Well, they found me, Suzy thinks. I
guess it pays to advertise.

Suzy drank and took the freeway
south with Matt for sex with Mark.
L.A., late at night, was muggy—
still quite warm but dank and dark.
Suzy thought about the people
sleeping in MacArthur Park.

Mark put on a leather collar.
Matt put on a leather vest.
Both had Suzy lick their pecs to
see who had the smoother chest.
By the morning, Suzy'd guessed that
Matt liked Mark—and Mark, Matt—best.

SUZY SINGS

Suzy leaves the car in Frisco,
by a hydrant in the Haight,
finds a spiffy travel agent,
Gordon's Good-as-Golden Gate.
Gordon has a sale on Europe,
says the fare is really great.

Suzy Zeus may die tomorrow.
Suzy Zeus may die tonight.
Suzy Zeus is taking over.
Suzy Zeus is taking flight.
Suzy's facing down the darkness.
Suzy's never burned so bright.

Suzy clambers uphill, downhill,
under bridge and over trench.
Sings all night beneath the redwoods,
lying on a cedar bench.
Sings a song for Bitterino.
Makes it up, with part in French.

Suzy's mind is branching. Suzy's
thinking at quadruple speed.
Bitterino. Carole King says,
I will follow where you lead.
Donnez-moi is "what I wish for,"
"hope for," "want," or, maybe, "need."

SUZY DOES BERLIN

Suzy Zeus is trying German.
Suzy Zeus is trying hard.
Passing with her sister's passport.
Paying with a credit card.
Suzy's putting up her hair, and
Suzy's letting down her guard.

Suzy's here to take the sights in.
Suzy's here to just unwind.
Suzy's here to feel her power,
here not just to search, but find.
Suzy's here to try the knockwurst.
Suzy's here to heal the blind.

Suzy drank a yard of *Weizen*
with a British guy named Paul.
Watched the eerie *Fernseh* tower
tower o'er the concrete Wall.
(British guys are British guys—if
you've seen one, you've seen them all.)

Suzy met a real live Jerry,
tall and bright-eyed, on a bike
—someone she could maybe care for,
someone she could maybe like—
with a thing for Proust and pastry:
Mee-kai-ELL, but call him Mike.

Mike and Suzy tried a disco,
and a bar, and Sacher torte.
Suzy, as her storm blew madly,
asked the waiter, Any port?
Eating, drinking, being merry—
live it up, 'cause life is short.

(Breathe) *Vergangenheitsbevelti-*
gung (it's best to say it fast):
it's a word from World War II—
to come to terms with someone's past.
Suzy climbed through bombed-out churches.
Even God can't make things last.

Mike says love is work, and worth it.
Suzy knows that love is luck.

Suzy wants to dance and drift, to
flow and flower, not get stuck.
Suzy doesn't want commitment,
doesn't want her life to suck.

SUZY IS A BERLINER

Suzy found a Hindu Buddhist,
lithe and lively, smart and small.
Saw him in *Der Rindfleischkeller*—
saved him from a barroom brawl.
Kissed her neck for two full hours.
Mendicants. They never call.

Suzy met a troupe of actors—
bored by fame, by raves, by hits.
Maybe Suzy lost her wallet,
maybe Suzy lost her wits.
Anyway, she woke up naked
next to their director, Fritz.

Freitag, in a German Shakespeare,
Suzy shivered in her chains.
Fritz had cast her as the ghost (with
bandages and bloody stains).
Suzy screeched and rolled her eyeballs,
blond and nubile, like most Danes.

In a slapped-together *Faustus*,
Greed and Lust and Sloth and Pride,
Gluttony, and Wrath, and Envy.
Suzy whispered, writhed, and cried.
Stroking Suzy, front and back, Fritz
shared his plans for suicide.

Shakespeare knew whereof he spoke—like
Hamlet, where the hero dies
after acting nuts all evening ...
What can you expect from guys?
Suzy needs an exorcism.
Suzy needs some exercise.

Suzy learned a lot of stagecraft.
Suzy even learned to act.
Suzy exercised her talent.
Suzy exercised her tact.
When the troupe ran out of money,
Suzy sighed, kissed Fritz, and packed.

CHAPTER 4
Suzy Back Home

SUZY PLANS

Suzy wants to make a baby.
Suzy can and Suzy will.
Suzy Zeus has had her fun now.
Suzy Zeus has had her fill.
Prick the condom, poke the cap, for-
go the sponge, forget the pill.

Suzy wants a changing table,
wants a playpen, blanket, crib,
booties, rattle, car seat, bottle—
matching high chair, spoon, and bib.
Suzy's had enough of working
and enough of women's lib.

Children hug you when you're chilly.
Plus they're cute and small and sweet.
Then they're good for when you're older.
Suzy likes their hands and feet.
Babies need you. Babies hold you.
Children make your life complete.

Last year Suzy had no warning.
This year Suzy's nice and calm.
This year's babe will be a blossom.
Last year's was a ticking bomb.
Suzy's got the formula—she's
ready now to be a mom.

Suzy needs to find a bouncer.
Suzy writes a classified
asking for a bodybuilder—
no one she's already tried.
Suzy puzzles over names. Cor-
vette. Pleshette. Ebonix. Clyde.

Sally's kids are Bobby, Sherman,
Cindy, Marcia, Archie, Jan.
All of them are tall and fair, ex-
cept for Arch, who's short and tan.
Keith has two. (Or five. But no one's
pinned it on him. No one can.)

Suzy, planning questions, plans on
knitting during interviews.

Come on, baby, be my music.
Come on, baby, be my muse.
Suzy wants an ethnic father
maybe. It's so hard to choose.

SUZY REVIEWS HER FINANCES

Suzy's pacing in her walk-up.
Suzy's going down the drain.
Suzy dreams of debtors' prison,
breaking rocks in ball and chain.
Suzy clenches, hears her mallet's
rhythmic pounding in her brain.

Suzy talked with Visa's cops, who
said she'd more than shot her wad.
Bit the bullet, called up Louie's,
got Joanne, and talked to Todd.
Suzy thought, The eight P.M. shift?
This can't be the will of God.

Maybe God's gone on vacation,
leaving everything to Fate.
What if everything is ruined?
What if He gets back too late?
Maybe she should move to Flushing.
Maybe she should move upstate.

Suzy needs a kid to kidnap.
Suzy needs a bank to rob.
Suzy needs a wealthy lover.
Suzy needs a high-paid job.
Let her win the lottery or
maybe just let loose and sob.

Suzy doesn't have a minute.
Suzy doesn't have a cent.
She would move if only someone
knew where Bitterino went.
Mrs. Tragas shakes her head: the
girlie didn't pay her rent.

SUZY TRIES THE TAO

Suzy's going slowly gaga,
wearing beads and making lists,
reads haiku, epistle, saga,
raises up her eyes and fists,
whispering a secret prayer
in case a god of God exists.

Suzy's going to shun samsara.
Suzy's going to give up sex.
Suzy's going to wear a sheet and
dance on Forty-third and Lex.
Suzy likes those guys with crosses
tattooed right around their necks.

Tsuzy wants to get enlightened.
Tsuzy wants to pierce her lip.
Tsuzy wants a new Taon jacket—
something holy, something hip.
Jazzed, Lao-Tsuzy meditates to
help her brain waves get a grip.

"Who can sit and watch the silt drift
down until the pond is clear?"
Suzy, groping, tries to downshift,
cannot find a lower gear.
Maybe she should read the paper.
Maybe she should buy some beer.

Suzy wants to be a mystic.
Suzy wants to read your palm.
Even though it's atavistic,
she's anointing folks with balm.
Suzy feels a bit ballistic
even when she's feeling calm.

Suzy walks, in Brooklyn, back and
forth along the Promenade.
On her windy roof she sings. The
neighbors act like Suzy's odd.
Suzy's whole and Suzy's wholesome.
Suzy Zeus is helping God.

Suzy's brain is spinning, sparking,
making meaning, waging war.
Tastes are mad explosions. Smells have
never smelled like this before.

53

Suzy's hot
then cold
then hotter.
Please don't seat her near the door.

Max-a-million Zeus-Rodriguez.
Lucy. Desi. Ricky. Kate.
No one's writing. No one's phoning.
Why is there no ready mate?
Suzy's full of grace, and blessèd.
It's so hard to knit and wait.

Suzy's actions act like arrows.
Suzy's speech is like a spear.
Suzy Zeus has saddened sadness.
Suzy Zeus has frightened fear.
Suzy's never been so happy.
Suzy's never been so clear.

Suzy's howling at her litter,
separating white from black,
separating good from evil,
separating from the pack.
Suzy Zeus is right on target.
Suzy Zeus is right on track.

SUZY TRIES THE DOW

Suzy Zeus has plucked her eyebrows.
Suzy Zeus has picked a goal.
Suzy has a new persona.
Sees life steady, sees it whole.
Suzy's going to get connected.
Suzy's going to get control.

Suzy smiles a ten-buck smile and
runs her finger down the list.
"Mr. Milken's here," she says, then,
"Have a seat." She flicks her wrist.
Finally, she's economic.
Suzy, Temp Receptionist.

Suzy wants a leather briefcase.
Suzy wants a silk-back vest.
Suzy doesn't need credentials,
but she'll get them, if it's best.
Suzy wants a window office.
Suzy wants her trousers pressed.

Suzy wants to buy a co-op,
put big art up on the wall.
Suzy wants to give some parties.
Suzy wants to give her all.
Suzy wants to be consulted.
Suzy's feeling ten feet tall.

Suzy wants a foreign nanny.
Suzy wants a private school.
Where they teach good manners and big
business and the golden rule.
Suzy wants a tennis camp, with
horses and a swimming pool.

All alone in blackness, Suzy
risks a little vertigo.
Pressed against the glass, she hears the
traffic moving far below.
Silent ballerina in the
office of the CEO.

SUZY FOLLOWS HER FEET

Money changing hands is evil.
Plastic's out, in any form.
Suzy knows to shed her jacket.
She can tell the evening's warm.
Suzy senses God among her.
Suzy smells the coming storm.

Suzy's stepping through the mirror,
stepping through a foreign land,
stepping through the grace of God, her
sandals in a stranger's hand.
Suzy rides another's power.
Nothing Suzy does is planned.

Suzy doesn't need direction.
Suzy uses dogs and trees.
Suzy's sensed a true connection
since she set aside her keys.
(Suzy put them in the clover,
careful signals to the bees.)

Suzy passes pickup soccer,
watches boys in cutoff jeans.
Corner kick—they're in formation,
information in the scenes.
Suzy sees it all so clearly.
Suzy wonders what it means.

Suzy climbs to reach the forest,
pinnacle of Prospect Park.
In the woods she stands and watches
as the borough swings to dark.
Sunset's when the devil beckons—
she can see him in the bark.

SUZY FOLLOWS HER FEET FARTHER

Suzy grips a sycamore, a-
waiting death, awaiting birth.
Hours. Waiting. Needs the sign to
show her value, prove her worth.
Suzy goes where Suzy's sent, to
do her job, to save the Earth.

Suzy Zeus is Agent Orange.
Suzy is an ammo round.
She's an AK-47
and its clacking, cracking sound.
Suzy is a combat unit.
Suzy is a battleground.

Suzy hosts a host of fighters,
demons some, some seraphim.
Suzy holds the broken pieces—
here a torso, there a limb.
Look for Suzy in the trenches.
Seek her where the light is dim.

Outside, Suzy's wild and wired.
Inside, Suzy's loud and loose.
Strangely, Suzy's never tired,
living now to be of use.
God has chosen certain people.
God is choosing Suzy Zeus.

Suzy's creeping. Night is sleeping,
dank and dark and stark and still.
Evil comes in many forms. She
wonders if she'll have to kill.
On the drive. A siren. Screaming
brakes—and racing down the hill.

SUZY FOLLOWS HER FEET
EVEN FARTHER

Three A.M. in deepest Brooklyn.
Shiny limos line the street.
Inside leather, silk, and spandex,
chains and lace and wine and heat.
Suzy's moving to the dance floor.
Suzy's moving to the beat.

Suzy slinks and Suzy gyrates.
See the sweat pour down her face.
Other dancers turn to watch her,
stop, and clap, and give her space.
Suzy, dance to save the moment—
dance to save the human race.

In the attic, after *Flipper*,
Barbie had to pay the price.
Skipper and the others watching,
Suzy chanted, rolled some dice,
stripped the virgin, struck the match, sat
back and made the sacrifice.

Barbie's hair was singed and smelly.
Barbie. What a stupid name.
Keith found Suzy in the crawl space,
told her there that if she came
out with him he'd give her gum. He
needed her to play the game.

Keith brought Suzy down the alley,
down behind the railroad grade,
down to where their sister, Sally,
waited in the birches. They'd
brought some string and scissors. Sally
told her not to be afraid.

Suzy doesn't wear a beeper.
Suzy's given up the phone.
Suzy bumps and Suzy shimmies.
Watch her muscles.
Hear her moan.

Suzy dances in the leaf mold.

Suzy dances all alone.

CHAPTER 5
Suzy Gets Religion

SUZY SLEEPS

Suzy's sleeping on the subway.
Suzy's sleeping on the 3.
Suzy's feeling like a wreck, a
bouncing check, a refugee.
Suzy needs a place to pray in.
Suzy needs a place to pee.

If you want a date with Suzy,
pin a carcass in your hair.
Wear a shark cage if you plan on
asking Suzy to the fair.
Suzy changes trains at Chambers,
since another train is there.

SUZY FOLLOWS HER FEET
INTO ST. JUDE'S

Hip-hop hymns are pounding madly.
Smell the smoke and feel the heat.
Candles glow and silver glistens.
Listen to that crazy beat.
Coney Island's now expanded
all the way to Hudson Street?

Look, it's Nathan's! In the narthex,
two-head fetuses in jars.
Down the aisle there comes a freak show—
someone's grilling rocks from Mars.
In her pew she wonders whether
all pews feel like bumper cars.

Some dumb merchant sold his holdings
all to buy one pricey pearl?
Suzy stays diversified, 'cause
Suzy's not that kind of girl.
Suzy tries to keep herself from
puking on the Tilt-A-Whirl.

"Step right up!" cries out one barker
from his sneaky ring-toss game.
Suzy pays, and plays, and misses
(gets a bunny all the same).
Suddenly she's on the Cyclone—
all she did was ask his name.

"Holy, holy," "God of power,"
"with our lips, but in our lives."
Suzy's engine's overheating—
it's enough to give her hives.
In the font she spys cool water.
Suzy takes a breath and dives.

Surfacing in Judah's Jordan,
seeing Baptist, seeing bird,
Suzy asks the man who's dripping
whose it was, that voice she heard.
Suzy wants to dwell among this—
she can be the flesh made word.

SUZY SAVORS PARISH LIFE

Suzy likes to read the Bible.
Suzy likes to smell its smell,
warm, spread-eagled there before her,
casting its unearthly spell.
Sometimes she pretends she's shut up
in her own monastic cell.

Suzy goes to church on Sundays.
Suzy goes to Evening Prayer.
Suzy goes to Bible study,
since the cute new rector's there.
(Suzy wants to press the vestments,
then decide what he should wear.)

Suzy'd like to hold the chalice.
Suzy'd like to pour the wine.
Suzy'd like to try a solo
antiphon (it's just one line).
Harry called her singing tone-deaf.
Suzy's singing is just fine.

Suzy wants to give a sermon,
mount and frame the parish quilt,
buy the wafers, clean the silver,
change the flowers when they wilt.
Suzy's going to be the biggest
pledger since St. Jude's was built.

Suzy wants to scrub the altar,
be there when the bread arrives,
help to push the boulder from the
doorway when our Lord revives.
Suzy likes the priests she's met. She
likes their husbands, likes their wives.

Life is back to normal somehow.
Suzy, safely in the flock,
thinks at thinking speed again and
sometimes sleeps around the clock.
Using towels and candlesticks, she
christens houseplants in her wok.

Suzy's been at church a month now,
shunning evil, doing good.

Suzy's looking up a passage
no one's ever understood.
Suzy loves not just her neighbors,
but the whole damn neighborhood.

SUZY PONDERS

Suzy used to feast on Sunday—
frosted flakes with milk, and toast,
juice and jam and steaming coffee,
then, pre-lunch, the wine and host.
Now, instead, she deeply tries to
teleport the Holy Ghost.

Suzy hears the organ starting,
shifts to sitting from her knees,
looks at all the pretty flowers,
wills a steady, cooling breeze.
(Last week Suzy tried the first row,
but the incense made her sneeze.)

Now Episcopalian, Suzy's
figured out what Jesus means:
buy a field and sow some seeds, rip
up the weeds, and eat your greens.
What does that new rector look like,
dressing up behind the scenes?

Suzy's ready for a mission.
This time Suzy won't go wrong.
Prospect Park was cold and dark, but
now she's better, calm and strong.
Still, she isn't great at waiting.
Hey, how long, O Lord, how long?

Suzy wants to grip life's passion.
Suzy wants to fight life's fight.
Suzy says to hell with fashion.
Suzy says to hell with fright.
Suzy says to hell with darkness—
Suzy says turn on the light.

Suzy hears the final reading
(how small is a mustard seed?),
pictures God as those beside her
stand and sing, and sit and read.
Suzy's dancing to the hymnal.
She's supposed to let Him lead?

SUZY PLEADS

Suzy, willing, waiting, isn't
liking what she's getting dealt.
God wants Suzy Zeus to cry, but
Suzy's not about to melt.
Wishes she could choke Him with the
rector's fancy bell-pull belt.

Suzy's feeling mighty lonesome.
Like a planet. Like a nun.
Like a hermit in his cabin.
Like a bad guy on the run.
Is it wrong if, now and then, she'd
like to have a little fun?

Suzy's feeling mighty timid.
Suzy's feeling mighty tense.
Suzy Zeus is mad, as ever,
that religion makes no sense.
Suzy's getting total silence
when she prays, or worse, repents.

Gazing at the congregation,
Suzy feels the men so near.
Half have muscles on their muscles.
So—invite them for a beer?
Half the congregation's gorgeous.
More than seven-eighths are queer.

Suzy gives to charities and
keeps their thank-yous on her shelf.
Suzy's been a sidewalk Santa,
raising funds—without an elf.
Suzy's done her part. Please note: she's
sick of being by herself.

Suzy thinks about the rector—
and that quiet deacon, too.
One is married, one's a homo.
What's a single girl to do?
Somewhere someone's there for Suzy.
God is gone, so tell her who.

SUZY PLUMMETS

Suzy wants to kiss the rector,
wants to lure him to her bed,
take him in the apse at night, or
in the aisle in church instead.
If God knew of Suzy's visions,
Suzy would be stricken dead.

Suzy sat and watched the Reverend
at her seventh Welcome Tea.
For a Father, Father Robert
was as hot as hot could be.
Now she hugs a sofa pillow.
Did he wonder? Could he see?

Robert does a lot of writing.
Robert knows a lot of art.
Once an Ivy League professor,
Robert is extremely smart.
Suzy's more than primed to give the
man her sacred bleeding heart.

Suzy Zeus has followed Robert
upstairs, downstairs, through the church.
He's so goddamn charismatic
he could end her guy research.
Suzy wonders what she looks like
from his lofty pulpit perch.

Suzy Zeus is cracking open,
tipping over, pouring out.
Suzy Zeus is spilling sideways,
falling faithward, dripping doubt.
Wants a little information—
like, to know what life's about.

Robert's gone to Massachusetts
in a sporty little car,
where, he says, there's only ocean
and a big ol' VCR.
Says he plans to rent some movies
then go biking wide and far.

Suzy Zeus, though left behind, is
trying hard to act adult:
not to grouse and not to gossip,

not to judge, condemn, insult.
Not to let herself start thinking
that St. Jude's is just a cult.

Suzy wants to wash his linens,
wants to hang out on his stoop.
Suzy wants to slash the tires
of his jazzy little coupe.
Suzy needs this priestly absence
as a moment to regroup.

SUZY TRIES NOT TO KICK HIM

Suzy Zeus could break his monstrance.
Suzy Zeus could burn his books.
Suzy may try *veritas*, and
soon—before she's lost her *lux*.
Suzy wants to bop him with his
secret practice bishop's crooks.

Suzy had a lunch of pasta
with the pastor of her dreams.
Suzy sat there silent, desperate—
counting floor tiles, waiters, beams.
Could he see her rigid posture?
Could he hear her inner screams?

Suzy wants to tell the preacher.
Suzy wants to take his arm.
Wants to make the congregation
raise its eyebrows in alarm.
Needs to come to (all) her senses—
not to hate him, not to harm.

Suzy Zeus, O perfect pinup!
Suzy Zeus, O perfect sphere!
Suzy Zeus, supremely sphygmic—
rhythm of my inner ear!
Suzy Zeus, so coeternal,
coincide and coinhere!

SUZY TRIES NOT TO CARE

Sometimes Suzy thinks that Robert
may be just a genius jerk.
Sometimes she could smash the windows
of his bonny Village kirk.
Face it—praying can't affect things,
and the Bible doesn't work.

Suzy's going to read the Tarot.
Suzy's going to cast the Ching.
Going to use the constellations.
Going to figure yan and ying.
Try out dream interpretation—
just like Martin Luther King.

Suzy wants a year of tangos.
Suzy wants a year of Scotch.
Suzy's going to speak, not listen.
Suzy's going to play, not watch.
Quite the eager beaver, Suzy's
back to bedposts she can notch.

Down at Louie's, Suzy needs a
skirt that gets her better tips.
For her birthday, give her leather—
something where the front unzips.
If she gets a telegram, it
better be a guy who strips. .

CHAPTER 6
Suzy in Love

SUZY MEETS A GUY

Last week, at a parish meeting,
Suzy saw a stunning sight:
someone with a brace of cheekbones
higher than a flying kite.
William spoke, and made it clear, on
top of that, that he was bright.

Bill knows port, and Bill knows starboard.
Bill knows booms, and ropes, and crews.
Bill can change his tack mid-harbor.
Bill knows all the microbrews.
Bill would like to take her sailing.
Bill begins to call her "Suze."

Bearded, tall, as thin as Jesus,
wowed by Christianity,
Bill has learned to work on water.
Bill gives Suzy rides for free.
Bill is into contemplation.

Suze prefers activity.

SUZY MAKES A DATE

Suzy Zeus is filling ketchups,
thinking that it's very Zen.
Killing time and killing roaches,
counting money, counting men.
Suzy wants to kiss and cuddle.
Suzy stops to wonder when.

Suzy's thinking back to Harry.
Looking forward to her date.
Will she get off work by "nine-ish"?
Will they keep her there too late?
Bill says call him, hey, whatever.
William's from the Lone Star state.

William's studied Being, Presence,
won't eat meat or wear real fur.
He's read Kant, a little Kafka.
Suzy thinks he's real mature.
Suzy wants to bear him presents:
gold and frankincense and myrrh.

William bought a Russian icon
for his roommate: angel, horn,
lily, dove, and seated girl—"To
you a baby will be born."
Suzy wonders if this handmaid
crops up in religious porn.

Suzy thought of Robert writing.
Suzy thinks of William bound.
Suzy thought of Robert reading
to himself without a sound.
Suzy thinks that Bill's the hottest
son of man for miles around.

Suzy wants his what and why. She
wants his when and wants it now.
Suzy wants his where and whether.
Suzy wants his who—and how.
Suzy wants a new communion:
bread and wine and *I and Thou*.

Suzy Zeus is mad about him
(let her sing it in the rain!)—

crazy for her handsome sailor
(spin and twirl, a weathervane!).
Suzy Zeus is full of feelings.
Suzy Zeus is feeling sane.

SUZY MULLS IT OVER

Suzy Zeus knows guys are shallow.
Suzy Zeus knows life is short.
Bill says let the field lie fallow,
bring provisions to the fort.
Suzy Zeus says ride the storm out.
Bill says shelter here in port.

Suzy wants a whole new haircut.
Suzy wants a special gown.
Suzy wants to wear silk stockings
and a boa and a crown.
Bill wears jeans and cotton T-shirts.
Bill is calming Suzy down.

Suzy hears but doesn't listen.
Suzy looks but doesn't see.
Suzy Zeus is like a chipmunk.
Bill is stiller, like a tree.
Bill knows how to stop and notice,
sit (or stand), and breathe, and be.

Suzy needs to slow her talking:
slow her teeth and tongue and lips.
Suzy needs to slow her walking:
toes and ankles, knees and hips.
Suzy needs to slow her radar:
slow the sweep and slow the blips.

Suzy watches Robert blessing,
bowing down, diluting wine.
Suzy tries to be a grape and
think of Jesus as her vine.
Tries to be an upright sheep, be
graceful as she waits in line.

Suzy's stance is so unsteady.
Suzy's grip is none too strong.
Suzy's feeling so unready.
Suzy's feeling so, so wrong.
Maybe this is just too heady.
This week's service is so long.

SUZY MAKES AN EFFORT TO
APPEAR PATIENT

Suzy Zeus is trying softball.
Suzy's trying macramé.
At first base and tied in knots, she's
at a loss for what to say.
All that she can think is, Will he?
All that she can do is pray.

Falling in makes love sound deep. A
vat. Or is it more an art?
Suzy's feeling scared and shaky
as she watches something start.
Suzy feels like someone's playing
table tennis with her heart.

Suzy pushes, pushes harder,
wonders where she wants to get.
Suzy isn't sure what's wrong, but
something hasn't happened yet.
Why is Suzy so unhappy?
Why is Suzy so upset?

Suzy tries to sit and wait for
matters slowly to unfurl.
Not o'ernight a grain of sand in
oyster doth become a pearl.
Suzy doesn't need a guy to
tell her she's a pretty girl.

Bill is loaning Suzy books to
look at while she's on the train.
Bill is making Suzy tapes, and
Bill is causing Suzy pain.
Suzy falls asleep to *Follies*
and the sound of driving rain.

SUZY MAKES AN EFFORT TO AVOID VIOLENCE

Suzy wants to take him sailing
just to smack him with the boom.
Suzy may just need to leave him
drowning in his elbow room.
Suzy wants to bean him with *The
Book of J* by Harold Bloom.

Suzy grants him room for elbows.
Suzy grants him room for knees.
Throw in houses while you're at it—
swing sets, cars, a couple trees.
He can find some other girlfriend.
Let her search for birds and bees.

Suzy has his number. Baby,
Suzy has his full address.
But how William thinks about her,
Suzy can't begin to guess.
Suzy, none too good at courting,
only knows the full-court press.

SUZY RETREATS

Suzy went beyond Poughkeepsie—
Suzy went to Holy Cross.
Looked and listened for the Lord, 'cause
Suzy knows the Lord's the boss.
Suzy went to shake her innards,
keep her soul from growing moss.

People try to contact God there.
People try the herbal teas.
People listen to their heartbeats,
to the wind through groves of trees.
Sometimes in the silence they re-
member where they left their keys.

Suzy gazed across the Hudson
at a mansion on a bluff,
trudged through trees and wet her knees—she
had to put on all new stuff.
Suzy's going to dance her praying,
like King David, in the buff.

Suzy met a handsome monk there.
Suzy met an aging nun.
Suzy asked the Holy Spirit—
and the Father, and His Son—
how to tell her own unconscious
from the Transcendental One.

When an insight comes to Suzy—
what to wear, or what to do—
could it be a gift from God, or
is it her? (They're not all true.)
Is the voice divine or human?
Suzy Zeus has not a clue.

Ancient Greeks, with nine to choose from,
sipped their ouzo, heard their muse.
Suzy wonders, was that real, or
was it maybe just the booze?
Suzy hears a thought. *His roommate
isn't just his roommate, Suze.*

CHAPTER 7
Suzy in Hell

SUZY CONSIDERS THE SITUATION

Suzy wants to kick his head in.
Suzy wants to hear him scream.
Suzy wants to lacerate him,
whack him with an iron beam.
Suzy's going to get revenge. New
ways occur in every dream.

Never last, or limp, or lazy,
always first, and fast, and fun,
now she's boiling, out for blood and
tears and sweat and number one.
Wishes she could get some bullets.
Wishes that she had a gun.

William stands beside his boyfriend.
By his boyfriend will he stay.
William stands to sing the hymns. He
sits to listen, kneels to pray.
How can William live without her?
She can change him off of gay.

At St. Jude's this balmy morning,
William's got a front-row seat.
Even way back by the organ
Suzy Zeus can feel his heat.
William's boyfriend looks like Ringo.
William's boyfriend can't compete.

Suzy Zeus is barely breathing,
still as stonework, mad and mean.
Suzy bows to sing the Sanctus.
Suzy's face goes gray, then green.
In her mind she tosses matches
into pools of gasoline.

William's boyfriend is a nebish.
William's boyfriend is a gnome.
Men can kiss in backstreet bars, but
men can never make a home.
William wants her. He's washed-up: a
Greenwich Village Ethan Frome.

SUZY CONSIDERS JUSTICE

Suzy's served the homeless homefries,
got them warm and got them fed.
Suzy's volunteered with kids. A
softball hit her in the head.
Suzy Zeus deserves attention.
Knows she should go back to bed.

Suzy Zeus is all for justice:
"As ye sow, so shall ye reap."
Hell was built for such as William—
men who dare make Suzy weep.
Suzy needs a team of lawyers.
Suzy needs a night of sleep.

Suzy's futon's full and fluffy.
Suzy's nightie's just like silk.
On the table by her bed, she's
got a little book by "Rilke"—
very deep, and good for sleep. She'll
count some sheep or warm some milk.

In the kitchen, whiskey sours,
sour grapes, and sauerkraut.
Suzy swimming, like a salmon,
upstream, driving, leaping out.
No, she knows she's hooked on William—
more like some dumb rainbow trout.

SUZY CONSIDERS MURDER

Suzy's living in a fishbowl,
in a fishbowl that's a font.
Living, through imagination,
what she's not supposed to want.
Feeling flattened, like a flounder.
Like those fans at Altamont.

William says it's called committed—
just like married, but for gays.
William says he's been acquitted,
says that Suze was just a phase.
Surely he's not that dimwitted …
Can't he feel her blood ablaze?

Suzy Zeus is his all over.
Suzy Zeus is his, all right.
Melting, boiling, steaming, Suzy's
glowing with a liquid light.
Suzy Zeus is his forever—
well, forever here tonight.

William's broken, like a record.
William's broken like a horse.
William's broken like a vacuum.
Get this man a gay divorce.
William sputters dots and dashes—
much like Samuel F. B. Morse.

Suzy's sure he's hiding something.
Suzy's sure—but God knows why.
Suzy, in the church hall kitchen,
hears him heave a heavy sigh.
William isn't going to kiss her.
Isn't even going to try.

SUZY CONSIDERS HER ROLE

Suzy's chest is cracked and hollow.
Suzy's muscles ache and strain.
Suzy's insides lie around her
on an open, windswept plain.
Suzy is an empty pelvis
and a burnt, exploded brain.

Suzy cannot walk on water.
Can't turn water into wine.
Can't make fishes into bread loaves.
Jesus can. In God's design,
God's the center. Is the church the
bride of Christ, or Frankenstein?

Suzy's always been important—
never some old also-ran.
Suzy's kept the whole world going,
since before the world began.
Where would Louie's be without her?
Who would take her shift?

Joanne.

SUZY CONSIDERS HERSELF LUCKY

Suzy Zeus saw Harry Sunday,
on the subway, in a suit.
Working on the Internet with
students, making loads of loot
teaching them communications.
(That, she thinks, does not compute.)

Harry had a better haircut.
Harry had a bigger place.
Suzy Zeus had vanished from his
daily life without a trace.
Suzy's going to write a novel:
Stupidheads in Cyberspace.

Harry'd learned a foreign language.
Harry'd found a lovely bride.
Harry'd opened up a business.
Harry'd traveled far and wide.
Harry'd seen her back at Louie's.
Harry'd seen her classified.

Harry cannot live without her.
Needs her there, a constant prop.
Look how hard he tried to hide that
minus Suzy, he's a flop.
Suzy sauntered from the train as
if she hadn't missed her stop.

SUZY CONSIDERS SUICIDE

Someone's standing in the bathroom,
staring into Suzy's eyes.
Someone with the look of voices
Suzy doesn't recognize.
Someone living in the mirror.
Some fat face that cries and cries.

Suzy's skull is packed and pounding.
Suzy's teeth are shaking loose.
Suzy's hands are slow and tremble,
covering the glass with mousse.
Suzy studied knots one summer.
Suzy doesn't know a noose.

Suzy feels a veil get lifted.
Suzy hears a veil get torn.
Then the truth lies, pinned, before her,
stark and struggling, woken, worn.
Hunger pangs are all that's certain,
all we're given when we're born.

SUZY TAKES A WALK

Suzy's crouching on the sidewalk.
Suzy's crawling in the street.
Suzy's weaving through the blackness,
catching headlights with her feet.

Suzy's tears are warm and tasteless.
Suzy's blood is hot and sweet.

CHAPTER 8
Suzy Committed

SUZY COMES TO

Rolling on a padded stretcher.
Someone says the taxi veered.

So, has she been hearing voices?

No, she thinks, just thinking weird.

Suzy's doctor wears a sweater,
brogues, a bookcase, and a beard.

SUZY CONFUSED

Suzy's roommates stare and mumble
on their creepy plastic cots.
Suzy's locked on Ten West A, a
safety zone ("no sharps, no hots").
Pencils at the nursing station,
no real vases, flowerpots.

Trying pills in sunset colors.
Some look like a smiley face.
Suzy's doctor shows her pictures
(modern artwork: messy ink).
Asks her first to count by sevens.
Panthers, bison, bats, a moth.

Suzy's thoughts are slow and sluggish,
Suzy's brain waves long and tall.
Asks her what the pictures look like.
Backward, down from eighty-one.
Suzy doesn't feel like moving.
There's no outlets in the wall.

SUZY CONFINED

Group is where they welcome Charlie.
Hair like wire, eyes like plates.
Calls himself a whirling dervish.
Says he's full of altered states.
Into Suzy's room at midnight
Charlie sneaks to read her Yeats.

Charlie's hushed and too excited.
Charlie's voice is moist and deep.
Charlie has a pair of glasses
like the headlights of a jeep.
Suzy wants to say good night now.
Suzy wants to go to sleep.

Love has built a castle somewhere.
Words come faster, lower, more.
Charlie speaks of Jove and Jesus,
heaven as "the farther shore."
Charlie brings up tears of joy and,
sobbing, rolls around the floor.

SUZY CONNECTS

Suzy Zeus got off the unit.
Said she needed space to pray.
In the chapel, Suzy read where
Jesus said "I'm in the way."
Then the priest arrived and blessed them.
Had them all sing "Day by Day."

Suzy feels a little better.
Suzy feels a little worse.
Suzy picks a favorite doctor.
Jim is Suzy's favorite nurse.

Jim thought church was really boring.

"Day by Day" has just one verse.

SUZY CONVALESCES

Every day she gets a menu—
dried-up pork, or dried-up steak?
Usually she asks for chicken.
Usually it's Shake 'n Bake.
Jim starts saving Suzy Jell-O,
squares of crumble, squares of cake.

Suzy's told to draw a picture:
"My Imagination Land."
Suzy has to sway in rhythm,
dance a color on demand.
Suzy bumps and grinds as purple.
Suzy draws a sun, and sand.

Jim says can he have the picture.
When she's discharged. Don't forget.
Jim says why's the beach towel empty.
Suzy hasn't got there yet.

Jim is into gene pools. Jim is
into genealogy.
Says that he's half Irish, which is
good to know, and good to be.
Says that Zeus is Greek, and that's the
reason Suzy loves the sea.

Suzy gets a pen from Jim. Draws
in a tiny ballpoint jet.

CHAPTER 9
Astroland

There's a loose in your walk
and a long in your bones
There's a scratch in your laugh
I'd like to own— own— own— own— own—

Donnez-moi your secretest secret
Donnez-moi your privatest part
Donnez-moi a new way of wishing
and I'll donnez-vous a place in my heart

There's a look in your smile
And the crook of your knee
There's a book on your bed
I'd like to be— be— be— be— be—

Donnez-moi a lick and a promise
Donnez-moi an umbrella you stole
Donnez-moi a new way of wishing
and I'll donnez-vous a place in my soul

Donnez-moi your silliest story
Donnez-moi your sharpest knife
Donnez-moi a new way of wishing
and I'll donnez-vous a place in my life

SUZY GETS OUT

Suzy's told to keep appointments.
Suzy's told, "Depression kills."
Suzy's told to keep good records.
Suzy's told to take her pills.
Suzy leaves the patient kitchen
with its plastic daffodils.

Jim has done some extra reading.
Zeus, he tells her, might be Dutch.
Zeus says thanks for care and feeding.
Jim says meds are not a crutch.
Jim tells Suzy keep on truckin'.
Jim tells Suzy keep in touch.

Suzy's tired in the taxi.
Suzy thinks about her bed.
Lithium's a heavy metal.
Suzy's arms and legs are lead.

SUZY GETS HOME

Sitting on the bathtub's edge. She's
here. She's her. She's back. She's out.
Fingering the splitting caulk, the
bathtub ring, the dirty grout.
Suzy's broken like a teapot—
cracked and glued but lost its spout.

Suzy wipes the messed-up mirror.
There she is: a second Eve.
Maybe just a little smarter.
Wonders what she might achieve.
Wonders if she has more bath salts.
Wonders, what does she believe?

Blessèd is she if she's crying?
Blessèd is she if she's poor?
Blessèd if she's hungry? Like her
floating soap, she's not quite pure.
Healing doesn't sound so finished.
God should grant an all-out cure.

Thank the Lord there's more hot water.
And her toes. She has all ten.
Suzy uses purple polish.
Has since grade school. Way back then.
Thinks about the Crucifixion
and the cruelty of men.

SUZY GETS SURPRISED

Suzy starts to read the paper.
Spends a lot of time in bed.
Rises slowly in the shadows,
kind of like a loaf of bread.
Suzy does some finger painting—
lots of blue with bits of red.

Suzy lies upon her sofa,
Suzy lies beside the phone.
Sometimes Suzy Zeus lies supine,
sometimes Suzy Zeus lies prone.
When it rings, it isn't William.
More like from the Twilight Zone.

Having saved the "Father Wanted"
from an ancient *New York Press*,
Bitterino, on a pay phone—
sounded like a total mess.
Suzy said to come and see her.
Said it was the same address.

SUZY GETS A RINSE

Suzy Zeus poured Bit some coffee.
Bit was looking awful low.
Like she had no pal to turn to,
like she had no place to go.
Needed food and needed friendship,
needed sleep and needed dough.

Bit wants change and wants it pronto.
Understanding's not enough.
What good's seeing what's repeating,
knowing it's the same old stuff?
Bit was tired, sad, and angry,
looking inward, looking tough.

Suzy has a long, long hallway.
Suzy has a rocking chair.
Still hears Harry where he isn't
(like, his footstep on the stair).
Bitterino brought her brushes.
Spent three days on Suzy's hair.

SUZY GETS GOING

Suzy's sleeping. Suzy's cooking.
Olive oil and lemon zest.
In the mirror Suzy's looking
at a friend from back out West.
Suzy's better.

                  Time to put her
higher powers to the test.

Suzy wants her line to God back.
Suzy wants to feel awake.
Suzy wants to feel a world that
isn't brave and new and fake.
Suzy ponders in her heart—can't
she control a manic break?

Suzy took her meds on Tuesday,
half on Wednesday, none today.
Suzy's mind is quicker now. To
take your pills and then to pray?
Stuffing earplugs in your ears. She
wants to hear what God will say.

SUZY GETS THE PICTURE

Father Robert preaches welcome,
action, risk, and ruthless love.
As she wanders, Suzy wonders
if it's this he's thinking of.
Suzy's lashed her soul to Him: the
talons on the Holy Dove.

Suzy nears the midnight Hudson,
where her pills will meet their fate.
Look—St. Jude's is full of candles.
Boy, St. Jude's is open late.
No one's shut the wooden doors, and
no one's closed the iron gate.

Sing, my tongue, the glorious battle,
Of the mighty conflict sing ...
Voices waft from all the windows.
In the yard the smell of spring.
Tell the triumph— Suzy enters.
Not much light ... *thy tribute bring.*

Rank on rank the congregation's
squeezed in tight beneath the dome.
This is like those crowds of tourists
visiting the Pope in Rome.
Then the hymn dissolves in silence.
Few by few the folks head home.

Everybody's very quiet.
No one laughs, or breathes a word.
Maybe she can ask on Sunday
what it was, the hymn she heard.
Suzy knows the people leaving.
Yes, she knows at least a third.

Dana's there, with Sam and Michael.
Lee is walking out with Tim.
Rachel must have had the baby ...
Hard to tell—the light's so dim.
William's boyfriend looks exhausted.
Steven's with the other Jim.

Toward the back, inside the chapel,
stands a special silver urn.
Burlap covers all the pictures.

Watchers watch the candles burn.
Could this be her mission starting?
Will her brain begin to churn?

People kneel, or sit, in silence.
Suzy wonders what they hear.
If they're hearing. Suzy wonders
if this happens every year.
God is there, but saying nothing.
Maybe not quite there, but near.

In the dripping of the candles
Suzy doesn't hear a call.
Suzy doesn't see a vision
in the wood grain on the wall.
Please don't let her task be small-time.
Please don't let her task be small.

Suzy prays to get directions.
Suzy prays to get a sign.
Suzy prays for more support: a
tougher shell, a stronger spine.
Suzy wants to battle evil—
things like war, and Columbine.

Then a wreck, a skinny neck, his
eyes a tangle, hair the same.
Suzy knows she knows those eyes, and
then she knows she knows his name.
Charlie, dressed to look dramatic.
Charlie looking pretty lame.

Trying hard to seem like lightning—
wanting silver, getting gray.
Jesus empty, not so frightening,
halfway through a Passion play.
Charlie's eyes are grasping fingers.
Suzy shrugs and looks away.

Suzy thinks of plastic stainless.
Who you are is where you've been.
Who you are is where you're going.
Maybe it's what shape you're in.
Maybe it's who's coming with you.
Are its edges at your skin?

Great. She's not just home but grounded.
Plus her homework may be dull.
Volunteering, at the church. Her

meds at work inside her skull.
It's no dove, the Holy Spirit.
Just a squawking common gull.

God may speak, but just to prophets.
Saints may, too, but just to Joan.
Suzy's not an island, but she
wanted so to work alone.
Suzy whacks the iron railings.
Suzy kicks the cornerstone.

SUZY GETS CURIOUS

Suzy reads the Dalai Lama.
Harry and the rest, go hang.
Suzy doesn't need more drama—
she's eschewing Sturm und Drang.
Robert says the world's not ending,
with a whimper *or* a bang.

March is Bitterino's birthday.
Suzy gets her ankle socks.
Tries to bake a flower cake the
shape of Bitter's favorite, phlox.
Devil's food with purple frosting—
pretty good for from a box.

John the Baptist baptized Jesus—
how can Jesus be a Jew?
Suzy can't fold down the kneeler.
Where's the goddamn pivot screw?
Should they sit? Will God be angry?
Move to someone else's pew?

Bitterino weighs the weight that
Suzy thinks is good to weigh.
Bit says Suzy's measurements are
absolutely quite okay.
Last night Suzy wondered if her
pubic hair would all go gray.

SUZY GETS READY

Signing up for singing classes.
Suzy's teacher's name is Nat.
Nat King Cole sang jazz like crazy.
Suzy wants to learn to scat
just like Ella (was it Billie?)—
first she's got to not be flat.

Suzy's going to train for choir
plus take lessons on her own.
Learn to breathe and count in quarters,
study Mozart, tune, and tone,
Gerald Near and all the Bach boys,
Calvin Hampton, chant, and drone.

SUZY GETS SOME FRIENDS

Suzy Zeus decides she'll try a
quiet pet, a pet that's calm.
Takes a single sleek, fat kitty
from the nearby yoga dham.
But her single, long-haired feline
soon becomes a single mom.

Suzy names the kittens Xanax,
Depakote, Alprazolam,
Paxil, Prozac, Tums, and Zoloft,
and she doesn't give a damn
that her shrinkie finds it "flippant."
He can turn his tail and scram.

Suzy lies there, late at night—the
kittens purr her favorite song.
Sleepy, Suzy slumps with all eight
feline friends to watch *King Kong*.
Suzy's in the dark about what
pals their mom has brought along.

Fleas like beds, and fleas like sofas,
underneath and up on top.
Suzy cannot use a swatter—
fleas don't fly so much as hop.
Suzy grabs the yoga mama,
crying, "No, this hell must stop!"

Suzy fogs, but still has insects.
Suzy fogs, and fogs times three.
Dizzy from the fumes she nearly
weeps when something bites her knee.
Mist and spray and powder follow.
Now, thank God, she's insect-free.

Suzy names the next ones Yahweh,
Adonai, and Elohim,
Jesus, God, and Holy Spirit,
El and Ba'al. In a dream,
all the kittens worship Suzy
every time she pours them cream.

SUZY GETS TO CONEY ISLAND

Bit is feeding Suzy grapefruit,
cantaloupe, and eggs on toast.
Suzy's eaten men for breakfast.
Suzy Zeus liked Brad the most.
Suzy likes to pedal downhill,
still not satisfied to coast.

Being bound's the only way, the
rector says, of being free.
More in Heaven, more on Earth, than
dreamt in your philosophy.
As she cycles, Suzy chooses
flat for distance. Helps her see.

Suzy can be strong and silent.
Suzy can be loud and weak.
Suzy's filling, Suzy's spilling,
Suzy's learning how to speak.
Suzy's falling like a sparrow—
grass and grammar in her beak.

Ocean Parkway ... ocean breezes ...
union with the bike she's on ...
red light ... green light ... Holy, Holy ...
Matt and Mark ... and Luke and John ...
Suzy checks the tomb and sighs. He's
just another guy who's gone.

Suzy's mind is slowly mending—
brains are, after all, just meat.
Knees and ankles ... Rhythmic bending
powers Suzy down the street.
Wonder Wheel. The journey's ending.
Suzy on her own two feet.

To her left, the Russian third-hand
thrift stores, where she wants to shop.
Straight ahead, that turning tower.
To her right, the rusted drop.
Someone died there, long ago, when
fun in free-fall didn't stop.

Suzy waits below the capsule
as it slowly rotates down,
buys a ticket, steps aboard, as-

cends. Manhattan's air is brown.
She can see the Chrysler Building.
She can see the whole damn town.

Suze revolves to face the ocean,
watches water swell and toss.
Thinks of her aborted mission.
Feels the power. Feels the loss.
Wonders, with enough confession
could she ever walk across?

T-shaped pier and wooden boardwalk.
Crabbers crab without a sound.
Suzy's level with the rusty
skeleton. She turns around.
Upturned faces near as she re-
turns to dusty, solid ground.

Suzy Zeus is making phone calls,
first to Jesus, then to Freud.
Suzy's writing invitations,
shouting questions at the void.
Suzy wonders where they are now—
all the men that she's enjoyed.

Suzy's singing on the mountain.
Suzy's silent in the mine.
Suzy's humming, making hash—and
pickles with her tears for brine.
Asking God to come for dinner.
Asking God to bring the wine.

Acknowledgments

This book owes its existence to Andrew Solomon, Suzy's oldest flame, biggest fan, and most exacting redactor. My gratitude to him knows no bounds. For their insight and support, I am greatly indebted also to Jeanne McCulloch, my editor; Jeff Posternak, my agent; and Christopher Ashley, Sarah Banks, Tom Beckett, Jude Biersdorfer, Tom Breidenthal, Christian Caryl, Max Cavitch, Dana Cowin, Robin Desser, Jennie Dunham, Ruth Ferguson, Roger Ferlo, Deborah Garrison, Robert Gottlieb, Anne Harlan, Liz Harlan-Ferlo, John Hart, Carol Henderson, Cheryl Henson, Elissa Lane, David Rakoff, Anne Richards, Pat, Rex, Tim, and Tory Robbins, Martijn Schot, Margaret Schultz, Amy Schwartz, David Shuler, Polly Shulman, Lucy and Priscilla Smith, Jim Standard, Tim Vasen, Greg Villepique, Howard Waldman, Mary Ellen Ward, Pete Wells, Susan Wheeler, Susan Wojtasik, and especially Joan Keener and Jaime Wolf. My final thanks go to Clay Shirky, for introducing me to Suzy in the first place.

A Note on the Author

Maggie Robbins is a psychotherapist living and working in New York City. With composer Robert Maggio, she wrote the libretto for the opera *Hearing Voices: Joan of Arc at the Stake*, which was performed at Pennsylvania's West Chester University. Her collages and assemblages have been shown from SoHo to Alberta and included in such books as M. G. Lord's *Forever Barbie: The History of a Real Doll*. She is fluent in Swahili. This is her first book.

A Note on the Type

Linotype Garamond Three is based on seventeenth-century copies of Claude Garamond's types, cut by Jean Jannon. This version was designed for American Type Founders in 1917 by Morris Fuller Benton and Thomas Maitland Cleland, and adapted for mechanical composition by Linotype in 1936.